BITE-SIZE
JANE AUSTEN

BITE-SIZE
JANE AUSTEN

Sense & Sensibility
from One of England's
Greatest Writers

COMPILED BY KARIN BAJI AND JOHN P. HOLMS

ST. MARTIN'S PRESS ❧ NEW YORK

THOMAS DUNNE BOOKS.
An imprint of St. Martin's Press.

Library of Congress Cataloging-in-Publication Data

Austen, Jane, 1775–1817.
　　Bite-size Jane Austen : sense & sensibility from one of England's greatest writers / [compiled by] Karin Baji and John P. Holms.
　　　　p.　cm.
　　ISBN 0-312-20501-5
　　1. Austen, Jane, 1775–1817—Quotations.　　2. Quotations, English.
I. Baji, Karin.　　II. Holms, John P.　　III. Title.
PR4032.B35　1999
823'.7—dc21
99-17699
CIP

First Edition: May 1999

10　9　8　7　6　5　4　3　2　1

To Tom, Pete, Matt and
all the rest on the 17th floor.
Thanks from us for all you do and
thanks, of course, from Lefty, too.

Contents

BITE-SIZE
JANE AUSTEN

ON SOCIETY

ON CHARACTER

Everything nourishes what is strong already.—*Pride and Prejudice*

There is a quickness of perception in some, a nicety in the discernment of character, a natural penetration, in short, which no experience can equal.—*Persuasion*

There are people, who the more you do for them, the less they will do for themselves.—*Emma*

Some wish, some prevailing wish is necessary to the animation of everybody's mind, and in gratifying this, you leave them to form some other which will not probably be half so innocent.

Like many other great moralists and preachers, she had been eloquent on a point in which her own conduct would ill bear examination.—*Persuasion*

After having much praised or much blamed anybody, one is generally sensible of something just the reverse soon afterwards.

Where so many hours have been spent in convincing myself that I am right, is there not some reason to fear I may be wrong?—Colonel Brandon, in *Sense and Sensibility*

ON CLOTHES & FASHION

To her, the cares were sometimes almost beyond the happiness; for young and inexperienced, with small means of choice and no confidence in her own taste—the "how she should be dressed" was a point of painful solicitude.—*Mansfield Park*

What dreadful hot weather we have! It keeps me in a continual state of inelegance.

We have been in two or three dreadful states within the last week, from the meeting of the snow, etc., and the contest between us and the closet has now ended in our defeat. I have been obliged to move almost everything out of it, and leave it to splash itself as it likes . . .

Miss Langley is like any other short girl, with a broad nose and wide mouth, fashionable dress and exposed bosom.

[Comments on a hat] I cannot help thinking that it is more natural to have flowers grow out of the head than fruit. What do you think on that subject?

I learnt to my high amusement that the stays [corsets] now are not made to force the bosom up at all; that was a very unbecoming, unnatural fashion.

Woman is fine for her own satisfaction alone. No man will admire her the more, no woman will like her the better for it. Neatness and fashion are enough for the former, and a something of shabbiness or impropriety will be most endearing to the latter.—*Northanger Abbey*

Dress is at all times a frivolous distinction, and excessive solicitude about it often destroys its own aim.

She lay awake ten minutes on Wednesday night debating between her spotted and her tamboured muslin, and nothing but the shortness of the time prevented her buying a new one for the evening. This would have been an error in judgment, great though not uncommon, from which one of the other sex rather than her own, a brother rather than a great aunt, might have warned her, for man only can be aware of the insensibility of man towards a new gown.—of Catherine Morland, in *Northanger Abbey*

ON COMPANY

"My idea of company," Mr. Elliot, "is the company of clever, well-informed people, who have a great deal of conversation; that is what I call good company."

"You are mistaken," said he gently, "that is not good company, that is the best."—Anne Elliot and Mr. Elliot, in *Persuasion*

Good company requires only birth, education, and manners, and with regard to education is not very nice.—*Persuasion*

One cannot have too large a party.—*Emma*

I hate tiny parties, they force one into constant exertion.

The sooner every party breaks up the better.—*Emma*

A watch is always too fast or too slow. I cannot be dictated to by a watch.—*Mansfield Park*

There was now employment for the whole party; for though they could not all talk, they could all eat. —*Pride and Prejudice*

I do not want people to be very agreeable, as it saves me the trouble of liking them a great deal.

You have delighted us long enough.—*Pride and Prejudice*

It was a delightful visit;—perfect, in being much too short.—*Emma*

A man who has nothing to do with his own time has no conscience in his intrusion on that of others. —*Sense and Sensibility*

[On a visit by well-born ladies] They called they came and they sat and they went.

ON CONVERSATION

I cannot speak well enough to be unintelligible. —*Northanger Abbey*

The usual rate of conversation; a few clever things said, a few downright silly, . . . nothing worse than everyday remarks, dull repetitions, old news, and heavy jokes.—*Emma*

Mrs. Allen, whose vacancy of mind and incapacity for thinking were such, that as she never talked a great deal, so she could never be entirely silent. —*Northanger Abbey*

Fair or not fair, there are unbecoming conjunctions, which reason will patronize in vain—which taste cannot tolerate—which ridicule will seize.—*Persuasion*

After long thought and much perplexity, to be very brief was all that she could determine on with any confidence of safety.—*Northanger Abbey*

Lady Middleton . . . exerted herself to ask Mr. Palmer if there was any news in the paper. "No, none at all," he replied, and read on.—*Sense and Sensibility*

[Preparing her sister Cassandra for a visitor] She has an idea of your being remarkably lively; therefore get ready the proper selection of adverbs, and due scraps of Italian and French.

The less said the better.—*Sense and Sensibility*

This is a very nice day; and we are taking a very nice walk; and you are two very nice young ladies. Oh! it is a very nice word, indeed! it does for everything. —*Northanger Abbey*

Elinor agreed to it all, for she did not think he deserved the compliment of rational opposition. —*Sense and Sensibility*

Here are we setting forward to spend five dull hours in another man's house, with nothing to say or to hear that was not said and heard yesterday, and may not be said and heard again tomorrow.—*Emma*

ON DANCING

Fine dancing, I believe, like virtue, must be its own reward. Those who are standing by are usually thinking of something very different.—*Emma*

It may be possible to do without dancing entirely. Instances have been known of young people passing many, many months successively, without being at any ball of any description, and no material injury accrue either to body or mind;—but when a beginning is made—when the felicities of rapid motion have once been, though slightly, felt—it must be a very heavy set that does not ask for more.—*Emma*

[Writing of a ball she attended] There was one gentleman, an officer of the Cheshire, a very good-looking young man, who, I was told, wanted very much to be introduced to me, but as he did not want it quite enough to take much trouble in effecting it, we never could bring it about.

ON FIRST APPEARANCES

There could be no doubt of his being a sensible man. Ten minutes were enough to certify that.—*Persuasion*

He was rather tall, had a pleasing countenance, a very intelligent and lively eye. . . . His address was good, and Catherine felt herself in high luck . . . when they were seated at tea, she found him as agreeable as she had already given him credit for being.—*Northanger Abbey*

From the first moment I beheld him, I was certain that on him depended the future happiness of my Life. . . . He did not speak; but I can imagine everything he would have said, had he opened his Mouth. I can picture to myself the cultivated Understanding, the Noble Sentiments, & elegant Language which would have shone so conspicuous in the conversation.—*Lesley Castle*

ON FLIRTATION

It was a child's play, chosen to conceal a deeper game.—*Emma*

Smiles of intelligence passed between her and the gentleman on first glancing . . . but it was most prudent to avoid speech.—*Emma*

This was a device, I suppose, to sport with my curiosity, and exercise my talent of guessing.—*Emma*

There is hardly any personal defect which an agreeable manner might not gradually reconcile one to.
—*Persuasion*

To be unaffected was all that a pretty girl could want to make her mind as captivating as her person.
—*Sense and Sensibility*

ON GOOD BREEDING

Sir Walter Elliot, of Kellynch-hall, in Somersetshire, was a man who, for his own amusement, never took up any book but the Baronetage, there he found occupation for an idle hour, and consolation in a distressed one.—*Persuasion*

She believed she must now submit to feel that another lesson, in the art of knowing our own nothingness beyond our own circle.—*Persuasion*

She was sometimes worried down by officious condolence to rate good-breeding as more indispensable to comfort than good-nature.—*Sense and Sensibility*

ON GOSSIP

Facts or opinions which are to pass through the hands of so many, to be misconceived by folly in one, and ignorance in another, can hardly have much truth left.

Call it gossip, if you will . . . something entertaining and profitable: something that makes one know one's species better.—*Persuasion*

Consequence has its tax.—*Persuasion*

Human nature is so well disposed towards those who are in interesting situations, that a young person, who either marries or dies, is sure to be kindly spoken of.—*Emma*

The ladies here probably exchanged looks which meant, "Men never know when things are dirty or not"; and the gentlemen perhaps thought each to himself, "Women will have their little nonsenses and needless cares."—*Emma*

To have been described long ago to a recent acquaintance, by nameless people, is irresistible.—*Persuasion*

For what do we live, but to make sport for our neighbors, and laugh at them in our turn?—Mr. Bennet, in *Pride and Prejudice*

Whenever I fall into misfortune, how many jokes it ought to furnish to my acquaintance in general, or I shall die dreadfully in their debt for entertainment.

One likes to hear what is going on, to *au fait* as to the newest modes of being trifling and silly.—Mrs. Smith, in *Persuasion*

You will have a great deal of unreserved discourse . . . I dare say, upon this subject, as well as upon many other of our family matters. Abuse everybody but me.

[Nurses] have great opportunities . . . Such varieties of human nature as they are in the habit of witnessing! And it is not merely in its follies that they are well read; for they see it occasionally under every circumstance that can be most interesting or affecting. What instances must pass before them of ardent, disinterested, self-denying attachment, of heroism, fortitude, patience, resignation; of all the conflicts and all the sacrifices that ennoble us most. A sick chamber may often furnish the worth of volumes.—Anne Elliot, in *Persuasion*

There is so much of gratitude or vanity in almost every attachment, that it is not safe to leave any to itself.

She was remarkably quick in the discovery of attachments, and had enjoyed the advantage of raising the blushes and the vanity of many a young lady by insinuations of her power over such a young man; and this kind of discernment enabled her, soon after her arrival at Barton, decisively to pronounce that Colonel Brandon was very much in love with Marianne Dashwood.—*Sense and Sensibility*

It is well known that Miss Manwaring is absolutely on the catch for a husband, and no one therefore can pity her for losing, by the superior attractions of another woman, the chance of being able to make a worthy man completely miserable.—*Lady Susan*

ON PUBLIC OPINION

We all have a better guide in ourselves, if we would attend to it, than any other person can be.

Where an opinion is general, it is usually correct.
—Mary Crawford, in *Mansfield Park*

One may as well be single, if the wedding is not to be in print.

There is exquisite pleasure in subduing an insolent spirit, in making a person predetermined to dislike, acknowledge one's superiority.—*Lady Susan*

ON WIT & RIDICULE

The wisest and best of men, nay, the wisest and best of their actions, may be rendered ridiculous by a person whose first object in life is a joke.—*Pride and Prejudice*

One cannot always be laughing at a man without now and then stumbling on something witty.—Elizabeth Bennet, in *Pride and Prejudice*

Wisdom is better than wit, and in the long run will certainly have the laugh on her side.

I hope I never ridicule what is wise or good. Follies and nonsense, whims and inconsistencies do divert me, I own, and I laugh at them whenever I can. —Elizabeth Bennet's claim to Mrs. Darcy, *Pride and Prejudice*

Mrs. Blount . . . with the same broad face, diamond bandeau, white shoes, pink husband and fat neck.

They had talked, and they had been silent; he had reasoned, she had ridiculed; and they had parted at last with mutual vexation.—*Mansfield Park*

It has been the study of my life to avoid those weaknesses which often expose a strong understanding to ridicule.—*Pride and Prejudice*

Such conduct made them, of course, most exceedingly laughed at; but ridicule could not shame, and seemed hardly to provoke them.—*Sense and Sensibility*

Her feelings are tolerably acute, and she is so charmingly artless in their display as to afford the most reasonable hope of her being ridiculed and despised by every man who sees her.—*Lady Susan*

On Men & Women

on men & women

One half the world cannot understand the pleasures of the other.—*Emma*

May I ask whether these pleasing attentions proceed from the impulse of the moment, or are the result of previous study?—*Pride and Prejudice*

With men he can be rational and unaffected, but when he has ladies to please, every feature works. —*Emma*

Of the subject I will only add, in justice to men, that though to the larger and more trifling part of the sex, imbecility in females is a great enhancement of their personal charms, there is a portion of them too reasonable and too well informed themselves to desire anything more in woman than ignorance. . . . a good-looking girl, with an affectionate heart and a very ignorant mind, cannot fail of attracting a clever young man, unless circumstances are particularly untoward.

I believe a true analogy between our bodily frames and our mental; and that as our [male] bodies are the strongest, so are our feelings; capable of bearing most rough usage, and riding out the heaviest weather. —Captain Harville, in *Persuasion*

All the privilege I claim for my own sex (it is not a very enviable one: you need not covet it), is that of loving longest, when existence or when hope is gone!—Anne Elliot, in *Persuasion*

We [women] live at home, quiet, confined, and our feelings prey upon us.—Anne Elliot, in *Persuasion*

In nine cases out of ten, a woman had better show more affection than she feels.

She was a woman of mean understanding, little information, and uncertain temper.—*Pride and Prejudice*

No one can think more highly of the understanding of women than I do. In my opinion, nature has given them so much, that they never find it necessary to use more than half.—Henry Tilney, in *Northanger Abbey*

In every power of which taste is the foundation, excellence is pretty fairly divided between the sexes. —*Northanger Abbey*

Next to being married, a girl likes to be crossed in love a little now and then.—*Persuasion*

GENDER DIFFERENCES

Maria, with only Mr. Rushworth to attend to her, [was] doomed to the repeated details of his day's sport, good or bad, his boast of his dogs, his jealousy of his neighbors, his doubts of their [hunting] qualifications, and his zeal after poachers—subjects which will not find their way to female feelings without some talent on one side, or some attachment on the other. —*Mansfield Park*

The Mr. Musgroves had their game to guard, and to destroy, their horses, dogs, and newspapers to engage them; and the females were fully occupied in all the other common subjects of housekeeping, neighbors, dress, dancing, and music.—*Persuasion*

ON A MIND MADE UP

Where the mind is perhaps rather unwilling to be convinced, it will always find something to support its doubts.

There is something so amiable in the prejudices of a young mind, that one is sorry to see them give way to the reception of more general opinions.—Colonel Brandon, in *Sense and Sensibility*

A persuadable temper might sometimes be as much in favour of happiness as a very resolute character. —*Persuasion*

He had learnt to distinguish between the steadiness of principle and the obstinacy of self-will, between the darings of heedlessness and the resolution of a collected mind.—*Persuasion*

Would Mr. Darcy, then consider the rashness of your original intention as atoned for by your obstinacy in adhering to it?—*Pride and Prejudice*

You know very well that my opinion would have no weight with you, unless it were on the side of your wishes.—Elinor Dashwood to Lucy Steele, in *Sense and Sensibility*

When the romantic refinements of a young mind are obliged to give way, how frequently are they succeeded by such opinions as are but too common, and too dangerous!—Colonel Brandon, in *Sense and Sensibility*

Like half the rest of the world, if more than half there be that are clever and good, Marianne, with excellent abilities and an excellent disposition, was neither reasonable nor candid. She expected from other people the same opinions and feelings as her own, and she judged of their motives by the immediate effect of their actions on herself.—on Marianne Dashwood, in *Sense and Sensibility*

ON ADVICE

It was, perhaps, one of these cases in which advice is good or bad only as the event decides.

Something occurred while they were at Hartfield, to make Emma want their advice; and, which was still more lucky, she wanted exactly the advice they gave.

Pardon me for neglecting to profit by your advice, which on every other subject shall be my constant guide, though in the case before us I consider myself more fitted by education and habitual study to decide on what is right than a young lady like yourself. —*Pride and Prejudice*

ON DINING OUT

There is, I believe, in many men, especially single men . . . a passion for dining out—a dinner engagement is so high in the class of their pleasures, their

employments, their dignities, almost their duties, that
any things gives way to it. . . . he cannot refuse an in-
vitation, he must dine out wherever he is asked.
—*Emma*

ON FLATTERY

Her humble vanity was contented—she felt more
obliged to the two young men for this simple praise
than a true-quality heroine would have been for
fifteen sonnets in celebration in her charms.
—*Northanger Abbey*

To say that Emma was not flattered by Lord Os-
borne's visit would be to assert a very unlikely thing,
and describe a very odd young lady; but the gratification was by no means unalloyed: his coming was a
sort of notice which might please her vanity, but did
not suit her pride; and she would rather have known
that he wished the visit without presuming to make
it.—*The Watsons*

From such commendation as this, however, there was
not much to be learnt; Elinor well knew that the

sweetest girls in the world were to be met with in every part of England, under every possible variation of form, face, temper, and understanding.—*Sense and Sensibility*

Friendship is certainly the finest balm for the pangs of disappointed love.—*Northanger Abbey*

But remember that the pain of parting from friends will be felt by everybody at times, whatever be their education or state.

We have been children and women together; and it is natural to suppose that we should be intimate. —*Emma*

The usual ceremonial of meeting her friend with the most smiling and affectionate haste, of admiring the set of her gown, and envying the curl of her hair . . . whispering to each other whenever a thought occurred, and supplying the place of many ideas by

a squeeze of the hand or a smile of affection.
—*Northanger Abbey*

ON HAPPINESS

Perfect happiness, even in memory, is not common.—*Emma*

Why not seize the pleasure at once? How often is happiness destroyed by preparation, foolish preparation?

I had a very pleasant evening, though . . . there was no particular reason for it; but I do not think it worth while to wait for enjoyment until there is some real opportunity for it.

A large income is the best recipe for happiness I ever heard of. It certainly may secure all the myrtle and turkey part of it.—*Mansfield Park*

No temper could be more cheerful than hers, or possess, in a greater degree, that sanguine expectation of happiness which is happiness itself.—*Sense and Sensibility*

A temper to love and be loved . . . must in any place, and any society, secure a great deal to enjoy.—*Mansfield Park*

Know your own happiness. You want nothing but patience—or give it a more fascinating name, call it hope.—Mrs. Dashwood to Edward Ferrars, in *Sense and Sensibility*

ON HEARTACHE

He was the first young man who attached himself to you. That was the charm, and most powerful it is.

But one thing may be said for me: even in that horrid state of selfish vanity, I did not know the extent of the injury I meditated, because I did not then know what it was to love.—*Pride and Prejudice*

Without shutting herself up from her family, or leaving the house in determined solitude to avoid them, or lying awake the whole night to indulge meditation, Elinor found every day afforded her leisure enough to think of Edward, and of Edward's behaviour, in every possible variety which the different state of her spirits at different times could produce,—with tenderness, pity, approbation, censure, and doubt.—*Sense and Sensibility*

She saw, as she assisted Marianne from the carriage, that she had been crying, she saw only an emotion too natural in itself to raise any thing less tender than pity, and in its unobtrusiveness entitled to praise.—*Sense and Sensibility*

ON HOW NOT TO ATTRACT A WOMAN

He said nothing worth hearing—looked without seeing—admired without intelligence—listened without knowing what she said.

Maria, with only Mr. Rushworth to attend to her, [was] doomed to the repeated details of his day's sport, good or bad, his boast of his dogs, his jealousy

of his neighbors, his doubts of their [hunting] qualifications, and his zeal after poachers—subjects which
will not find their way to female feelings without some
talent on one side, or some attachment on the other.—
Mr. Rushworth to Maria Bertram, *Mansfield Park*

John Thorpe . . . was a stout young man of middling
height, who, with a plain face and ungraceful form,
seemed fearful of being too handsome unless he wore
the dress of a groom, and too much like a gentleman
unless he were easy where he ought to be civil, and
impudent where he might be allowed to be easy.
—John Thorpe to Catherine Morland, *Northanger
Abbey*

She followed him in all his admiration as well as
she could. To go before or beyond him was impossible . . . she could strike out nothing new in commendation, but she readily echoed whatever he chose to
assert, and it was finally settled between them without
any difficulty that his equipage was altogether the
most complete of its kind in England, his carriage the
neatest, his horse the best goer, and himself the best
coachman.

All the rest of his conversation, or rather talk, began and ended with himself and his own concerns.

You must give me leave to flatter myself that your re-fusal of my addresses is merely words of course. My reasons for believing it are briefly these: It does not appear to me that the establishment I can offer would be any other than highly desirable; and you should take it into farther consideration that in spite of your manifold attractions, it is by no means certain that another offer of marriage may ever be made you. Your portion [wealth] is unhappily so small that it will in all likelihood undo the effects of your loveliness and amiable qualifications. As I must therefore conclude that you are not serious in your rejection of me, I shall choose to attribute it to your wish of increasing my love by suspense, according to the usual practice of elegant females.—Mr. Collins to Elizabeth Bennet, in *Pride and Prejudice,* after she has several times tried to convince him that she is serious in turning down his proposal of marriage

A second attachment is seldom attended with any serious consequences; against that therefore I have nothing to say. Preserve yourself from a first love and you need not fear a second.—*Jack and Alice*

Matrimony, as the origin of change, was always disagreeable.—*Emma*

Anything is to be preferred or endured rather than marrying without affection.

It is always incomprehensible to a man that a woman should ever refuse an offer of marriage.

A lady's imagination is very rapid; it jumps from admiration to love, from love to matrimony in a moment.—*Pride and Prejudice*

No young lady can be justified in falling in love before the gentleman's love is declared.—*Northanger Abbey*

There is not one in a hundred of either sex who is not taken in when they marry. Look where I will, I see that it is so; and I feel that it must be so, when I consider that it is, of all transactions, the one in which people expect most from others, and are the least honest themselves.—*Mansfield Park*

I should deserve utter contempt if I dared to suppose that true attachment and constancy were known only by woman. No, I believe you [men] capable of everything great and good in your married lives . . . so long as you have an object. I mean while the woman you love lives, and lives for you.—Anne Elliot, in *Persuasion*

Dr. Gardiner was married yesterday to Mrs. Percy and her three daughters.

I shall not be a poor old maid, and it is poverty only which makes celibacy contemptible to a generous public!—*Emma*

It is a truth universally acknowledged, that a single man in possession of a good fortune, must be in want of a wife.—*Pride and Prejudice*

A single woman of good fortune, is always respectable, and may be as sensible and pleasant as anybody else.—*Emma*

An engaged woman is always more agreeable than a disengaged. She is satisfied with herself. Her cares are over, and she feels that she may exert all her powers of pleasing without suspicion. All is safe with a lady engaged; no harm can be done.—Henry Crawford, in *Mansfield Park*

It is better to know as little as possible of the defects of the person with whom you are to pass your life. —*Pride and Prejudice*

Where people wish to attach, they should always be ignorant. To come with a well-informed mind, is to come with an inability of administering to the vanity of others, which a sensible person would always wish to avoid.—*Northanger Abbey*

Seven years would be insufficient to make some people acquainted with each other, and seven days are more than enough for others.—*Sense and Sensibility*

Happiness in marriage is entirely a matter of chance.—*Pride and Prejudice*

When any two young people take it into their heads to marry, they are pretty sure by perseverance to carry their point, be they ever so poor, or ever so imprudent, or ever so little likely to be necessary to each other's ultimate comfort.—*Persuasion*

Suitableness as companions; a suitableness which comprehended health and temper to bear inconveniences—cheerfulness to enhance every pleasure—and affection and intelligence, which might supply it among themselves it there were disappointments abroad.—*Pride and Prejudice*

Single women have a dreadful propensity for being poor, which is one very strong argument in favour of matrimony.

Handsome young men must have something to live on, as well as the plain.

What is the difference, in matrimonial affairs, between the mercenary and the prudent motive?—Elizabeth Bennet to Mrs. Gardiner, in *Pride and Prejudice*

Dr. Gardiner was married yesterday to Mrs. Percy and her three daughters.

Eliza Bennet is one of those young ladies who seek to recommend themselves to the other sex by undervaluing their own, and with many men, I dare say, it succeeds. But, in my opinion, it is a paltry device, a very mean art.—Caroline Bingley to Darcy, in *Pride and Prejudice*

People that marry can never part, but must go and keep house together.—Catherine Morland defines matrimony for Henry Tilney, in *Northanger Abbey*

"Ay, you may abuse me as you please," said the good-natured old lady; "you have taken Charlotte off my hands, and cannot give her back again. So there I have the whip hand of you."—Mrs. Jennings addresses her son-in-law, in *Sense and Sensibility*

ON MEMORY

There seems something more speakingly incomprehensible in the powers, the failures, the inequalities of memory, than in any other of our intelligences. The memory is sometimes so retentive, so serviceable, so obedient—at others, so bewildered and so weak— and at others again, so tyrannic, so beyond control. —*Mansfield Park*

My feelings are not quite so evanescent, nor my memory of the past under such easy dominion as one finds to be the case with men of the world.—*Mansfield Park*

How wonderful, how very wonderful the operations of time, and the changes of the human mind! If any one faculty of our nature may be called more wonderful than the rest, I do think it is memory.—*Mansfield Park*

The sweet scenes of autumn were for a while put by, unless some tender sonnet, fraught with the apt analogy of the declining year, with declining happiness, and the images of youth and hope, and spring, all gone together, blessed her memory.—*Persuasion*

He may live in my memory as the most amiable man of my acquaintance, but that is all.—*Pride and Prejudice*

But in such cases as these, a good memory is unpardonable.—*Pride and Prejudice*

Her mind was inevitably at liberty; her thoughts could not be chained elsewhere; and the past and the future, on a subject so interesting, must be before her, must force her attention, and engross her memory, her reflection, and her fancy.—*Sense and Sensibility*

She was nothing more than a mere good-tempered, civil and obliging young woman; as such we could scarcely dislike her—she was only an object of contempt.

We do not look in great cities for our best morality.

She had been forced into prudence in her youth, she learned romance as she grew older—the natural sequel of an unnatural beginning.—*Persuasion*

Loss of virtue in a female is irretrievable . . . one false step involves her in endless ruin.—*Pride and Prejudice*

Seldom, very seldom, does complete truth belong to any human disclosure; seldom can it happen that something is not a little disguised, or a little mistaken.—*Emma*

I will not say that your mulberry trees are dead, but I am afraid they are not alive.

In the principal facts they [histories] have sources of intelligence in former histories and records, which may be as much depended on, I conclude, as anything that does not actually pass under one's own observation.—*Northanger Abbey*

A woman especially, if she have the misfortune of knowing anything, should conceal it as well as she can.

Nothing is more deceitful than the appearance of humility. It is often only carelessness of opinion, and sometimes an indirect boast.—Darcy, in *Pride and Prejudice*

ON SHYNESS & RESERVE

What is become of all the shyness in the world?

There is safety in reserve, but no attraction. One cannot love a reserved person.—Frank Churchill, in *Emma*

Not till the reserve ceases towards one's self; and then the attraction may be the greater.—Emma responds to Frank Churchill, in *Emma*

She could so much more depend upon the sincerity of those who sometimes looked or said a careless or a hasty thing, than those whose presence of mind never varied, whose tongue never slipped. —*Persuasion*

Shyness is only the effect of a sense of inferiority in some way or other.—*Sense and Sensibility*

He was shy, and disposed to abstraction.—*Persuasion*

If I could persuade myself that my manners were perfectly easy and graceful, I should not be shy.—*Sense and Sensibility*

Georgiana's reception of them was very civil; but attended with all that embarrassment which, though proceeding from shyness and the fear of doing wrong, would easily give to those who felt themselves inferior the belief of her being proud and reserved.—*Pride and Prejudice*

I never wish to offend, but I am so foolishly shy, that I often seem negligent, when I am only kept back by my natural awkwardness.—*Sense and Sensibility*

She had heard that Miss Darcy was exceedingly proud; but the observation of a very few minutes convinced her that she was only exceedingly shy.—*Pride and Prejudice*

On the Arts & Writing

On Writing Novels

I wrote without much effort, for I was rich, and the rich are always respectable, whatever be their style of writing.

I . . . do not think the worse of him for having a brain so very different from mine. . . . And he deserves better treatment than to be obliged to read any more of my works.

An artist cannot do anything slovenly.

I may boast myself to be, with all possible vanity, the most unlearned and uninformed female who ever dared to be an authoress.

[Jane writes to tell her sister Cassandra that she received her first copy of *Pride and Prejudice,* misquoting Sir Walter Scott's *Marmion*] I want to tell you that I have got my own darling child from London. . . . there are a few typical errors—and a "said he" or a "said she" would sometimes make the dialogue more immediately clear—but "I do not write for such dull elves / As have not a great deal of ingenuity themselves."

[On the use of her name on the publication of her third book; her first two books were published anonymously] The truth is that the secret has so far as to be scarcely the shadow of a secret now and that I believe whenever the third appears, I shall not even attempt to tell lies about it, I shall rather try to make all the money than all the mystery I can of it. People shall pay for their knowledge if I can make them.

[Writing to the Prince Regent's librarian, about possible patronage by the House of Saxe-Coborg] I am fully sensible that an historical romance, founded on the House of Saxe-Coborg, might be much more to the purpose of profit or popularity than such pictures of domestic life in country villages as I deal in—but I could no more write a romance than an epic poem. . . . No, I must keep to my own style and go on in my own way; and though I may never succeed again in that, I am convinced that I should totally fail in any other.

I could not sit seriously down to write a serious romance under any other motive than to save my life, and if it were indispensable for me to keep it up and never relax into laughing at myself or at other people, I am sure I should be hung before I had finished the first chapter.

I write only for fame, and without any view to pecuniary emolument.

[Visiting London as a successful author] I liked my solitary elegance very much and was ready to laugh all the time at my being where I was. I could not but feel that I had a naturally small right to be parading about London in a barouche.

People are more ready to borrow and praise, than to buy—which I cannot wonder at; but though I like praise as well as anybody, I like what Edward calls *Pewter* too.

Walter Scott has no business to write novels, especially good ones. It is not fair. He has fame and profit enough as a poet, and should not be taking the bread out of other people's mouths.

[On the character of Elizabeth Bennet] I must confess that I think her as delightful a creature as ever appeared in print, and how I shall be able to tolerate those who do not like her at least, I do not know.

The work is rather too light and bright and sparkling; it wants shade; it wants to be stretched out here and there with a long chapter—of sense it could be had; if not, of solemn specious nonsense—about something unconnected with the story; an essay on writing, a critique on Sir Walter Scott, or the history of Bonaparté, or anything that would form a contrast, and bring the reader with increased delight to the playfulness and epigrammatism of the general style.

[Offering criticism to her niece and aspiring novelist, Anna Austen] Let the Portmans go to Ireland, but as you know nothing of the manners there, you had better not go with them. You will be in danger of giving false representations. . . .

. . . You are now collecting your people delightfully, getting them exactly into such a spot as is the delight of my life. Three or four families in a country village is the very thing to work on.

[Teasing her young nephew, James Edward, about his current experiment in novel writing] What should I do with your strong, manly, spirited sketches, full of variety and glow? How could I possibly join them on to the little bit (two inches wide) of ivory on which I work with so fine a brush, as produces little effect after much labour?

ON BOOKS & GENDER

I do not think I ever opened a book in my life which had not something to say upon woman's inconstancy. . . . But perhaps you will say, these were all written by men.—Captain Harville to Anne Elliot, in *Persuasion*

Anne replies to Captain Harville—
      . . . if you please, no reference to examples in books. Men have had every advantage of us in telling their own story. Education has been theirs in so much higher a degree; the pen has been in their hands. I will not allow books to prove anything.

I often wonder how you can find time for what you do, in addition to the care of the house; and how good Mrs. West could have written such books and collected so many hard works, with all her family cares, is still more a matter of astonishment! Composition seems to me impossible with a head full of joints of mutton and doses of rhubarb.

ON CORRESPONDENCE

Expect a most agreeable letter, for not being overburdened with subject, I shall have no check to my genius from beginning to end.

Your silence on the subject . . . makes me suppose your curiosity too great for words.

A person who can write a long letter with ease, cannot write ill.—Mrs. Bingley, in *Pride and Prejudice*

The post-office is a wonderful establishment! The regularity and dispatch of it! If one thinks of all that it has to do, and all that it does so well, it is really astonishing!—*Emma*

I assure you I am as tired of writing long letters as you can be. What a pity that one should still be so fond of receiving them!

You deserve a longer letter than this; but it is my un-happy fate seldom to treat people so well as they de-serve.

She is probably by this time as tired of me, as I am of her; but as she is too polite and I am too civil to say so, our letters are still as frequent and affectionate as ever.—*Lesley Castle*

Fanny Austen's match is quite news, and I am sorry she has behaved so ill. There is some comfort to us in her misconduct, that we have not a congratulatory letter to write.

Everybody allows that the talent of writing agreeable letters is peculiarly female. . . . The usual style of let-ter writing among women is faultless, except in three particulars: a general deficiency of subject, a total inattention to stops, and a very frequent ignorance of grammar.—Henry Tilney, in *Northanger Abbey*

I have now attained the true art of letter-writing, which we are always told, is to express on paper exactly what one would say to the same person by word of mouth; I have been talking to you almost as fast as I could the whole of this letter.

Literature

You describe a sweet place, but your descriptions are often more minute than would be liked. You give too many descriptions of right hand and left.

I will improve upon [self-control];—my heroine shall not merely be wafted down an American river in a boat by herself, she shall cross the Atlantic in the same way.

He and I should not in the least agree of course, in our idea of novels and heroines;—pictures of perfection as you know make me sick and wicked.

Let other pens dwell on guilt and misery. I quit such odious subjects as soon as I can.

Only a novel! . . . only some work in which the greatest powers of the mind are displayed, in which the most thorough knowledge of human nature, the happiest delineation of its varieties, the liveliest effusions of wit and humour, are conveyed to the world in the best-chosen language.—*Northanger Abbey*

"I never look at it," said Catherine, as they walked along the side of the river, "without thinking of the south of France."

"You have been abroad then?" said Henry, a little surprised.

"Oh no!, I only mean what I have read about." —*Northanger Abbey*

The person, be it gentleman or lady, who has not pleasure in a good novel, must be intolerably stupid!—*Northanger Abbey*

Provided they were all story and no reflection, she had never any objection to books at all.—of Catherine, *Northanger Abbey*

I am afraid [he] will be too much in the common novel style—a handsome, amiable, unexceptional young man (such as do not much abound in real life) desperately in love, and all in vain.

Poetry

I have read several of Burns's poems with great delight but I am not poetic enough to separate a man's poetry entirely from his character; and poor Burns's known irregularities greatly interrupt my enjoyment of his lines. I have difficulty in depending on the truth of his feelings as a lover. I have not faith in the sincerity of the affections of a man of his description. He felt and he wrote and he forgot.—Charlotte Heywood, in *Sandition*

I wonder who first discovered the efficacy of poetry in driving away love!—*Pride and Prejudice*

[A mock lyric on Reading in the Newspapers of the Marriage of Mr. Gell to Miss Gill]

At Eastbourne Mr. Gell, From being perfectly well,
Became dreadfully ill, For love of Miss Gill.
So he said with some sighs, I'm the slave of your iis;
Oh, restore, if you please, By accepting my ees.

He repeated, with such tremulous feeling, the various lines which imaged a broken heart, or a mind destroyed by wretchedness, and looked so entirely as if he meant to be understood, that she ventured to hope he did not always read only poetry, and to say, that she thought it was the misfortune of poetry to be seldom safely enjoyed by those who enjoyed it completely; and that the strong feelings which alone could estimate it truly were the very feelings which ought to taste it but sparingly.—*Persuasion*

He was evidently a young man of considerable taste in reading, though principally in poetry; and besides the persuasion of having given him at least an evening's indulgence in the discussion of subjects . . . she had the hope of being of real use to him in some suggestions as to the duty and benefit of struggling against affliction, which had naturally grown out of their conversation.—*Persuasion*

He would gain cheerfulness, and she would learn to be an enthusiast for Scott and Lord Byron; nay, that was probably learnt already; of course they had fallen in love over poetry.—*Persuasion*

This is nearly the sense, or rather the meaning of the words, for certainly the sense of an Italian love-song must not be talked of, but it is as nearly the meaning I can give; for I do not pretend to understand the language.—Anne Elliot, in *Persuasion*

ON READING

When thought had been freely indulged, in contrasting the past and the present, the employment of mind and dissipation of unpleasant ideas which only reading could produce made her thankfully turn to a book.—*The Watsons*

Provided that nothing like useful knowledge could be gained from them, provided they were all story and no reflection, she had never any objection to books at all.—*Northanger Abbey*

With a book, he was regardless of time.—*Pride and Prejudice*

[Lady Middleton reflects on Emma and Marianne in *Sense and Sensibility*] . . . because they were fond of reading she fancied them satirical: perhaps without exactly knowing what it was to be satirical.

ON HAPPY ENDINGS

The anxiety, which in this state of their attachment must be the portion of Henry and Catherine, and of all who loved either, as to its final event, can hardly extend, I fear, to the bosom of my readers, who will see in the tell-tale compression of the pages before them, that we are all hastening together to perfect felicity.—*Northanger Abbey*

ON BUSINESS & POLITICS

ON EMPLOYMENT

Mine is an active, busy mind, with a great many independent resources; and I do not perceive why I should be more in want of employment at forty or fifty than one-and-twenty.—*Emma*

There is nothing like employment, active indispensable employment, for relieving sorrow.—*Mansfield Park*

Employment, even melancholy, may dispel melancholy.—*Mansfield Park*

The money is nothing, it is not an object, but employment is the thing.—*Northanger Abbey*

A submissive spirit might be patient, a strong understanding would supply resolution, but here was something more; here was that elasticity of mind, that disposition to be comforted, that power of turning readily from evil to good, and of finding employment which carried her out of herself, which was from nature alone.—*Persuasion*

I must have employment and society.—*Pride and Prejudice*

It has been, and is, and probably will always be, a heavy misfortune to me, that I have had no necessary business to engage me, no profession to give me employment, or afford me any thing like independence.—*Sense and Sensibility*

It shall be regulated, it shall be checked by religion, by reason, by constant employment.—*Sense and Sensibility*

ON MONEY & BUSINESS

Business, you know, may bring money, but friendship hardly ever does.—John Knightley, in *Emma*

Success supposes endeavour.—*Emma*

An annuity is a very serious business.—*Sense and Sensibility*

I am afraid that the pleasantness of an employment does not always evince its propriety.—Elinor, in *Sense and Sensibility*

It is for your children's good that I wish to be richer.—*Mansfield Park*

From politics, it was an easy step to silence.
—*Northanger Abbey*

My poor aunt had certainly little cause to love the state; but, however, speaking from my own observation, it is a maneuvering business.—*Mansfield Park*

You [men] have politics, of course; and it would be too bad to plague you with the names of people and parties that fill up my time.

ON ENGLAND

ON HISTORY

History, real solemn history, I cannot be interested in. . . . I read it a little as a duty; but it tells me nothing that does not either vex or weary me. The quarrels of popes and kings, with wars and pestilences in every page; the men all so good for nothing, and hardly any women at all.—Catherine Morland, in *Northanger Abbey*

I often think it odd that [history] should be dull, for a great deal of it must be invention. The speeches that are put into the heroes' mouths, their thoughts and designs—the chief of all this must be invention, and invention is what delights me in other books.
—Catherine Morland, in *Northanger Abbey*

ON THE HISTORY OF ENGLAND

The history of England from the Reign of Henry IV to the Death of Charles I (from a childhood journal)

By a partial, prejudiced and ignorant historian
N.B. There will be very few Dates in this History

One of Edward's [Edward IV] mistresses was Jane Shore, who has had a play written about her, but it is a tragedy and therefore not worth reading.

[Henry VI] married Margaret of Anjou, a woman whose distress and misfortunes were so great as almost to make me who hated her, pity her.

His majesty died and was succeeded by his son Henry [VII] whose only merit was his not being *quite* so bad as his daughter Elizabeth.

[On Henry VIII] Nothing can be said in his vindication, but that his abolishing Religious Houses and leaving them to the ruinous depredations of time has been of infinite use to the landscape of England in general.

[On the Duke of Somerset, Protector of the Realm during the youth of Edward VI] He was beheaded, of which he might with reason have been proud.

Lady Jane Grey, who though inferior to her lovely cousin [Mary] the Queen of Scots, was as yet an amiable young woman and famous for reading Greek while other people were hunting.

[Lady Jane Grey] preserved the same appearance of knowledge and contempt of what was generally esteemed pleasure, during the whole of her life, for she declared herself displeased with being appointed Queen, and while conducting to the scaffold, she wrote a sentence in Latin and another in Greek on seeing the dead body of her husband accidentally passing that way.

[On Queen Mary] Nor can I pity the kingdom for the misfortunes they experienced during her reign, since they fully deserved them, for having allowed her to succeed her brother—which was a double piece of folly, since they might have foreseen that as she died without children, she would be succeeded by that disgrace to humanity, that pest of society, Elizabeth.

[On the reign of James I] As I am myself partial to the Roman Catholic religion, it is with infinite regret that I am obliged to blame the behaviour of any member of it: yet Truth being I think very excusable in an historian, I am necessitated to say that in this reign the Roman Catholics of England did not behave like gentlemen to the Protestants. Their behaviour indeed to the royal family and both houses of Parliament might justly be considered by them as very uncivil.

[On Charles I] this amiable monarch seems born to have suffered misfortunes equal to those of his lovely grandmother [Mary]; Misfortunes which he could not deserve since he was her descendant.

The events of this reign [of Charles I] are too numerous for my pen, and indeed the recital of any events (except what I make myself) is uninteresting to me; my principal reason for undertaking the History of England being to prove the innocence of the Queen of Scotland, which I flatter myself with having effectually done, and to abuse Elizabeth.

ON ENGLAND & ENGLISHMEN

I hope your letters from abroad are satisfactory. They would not be satisfactory to me, I confess, unless they breathed a strong spirit of regret for not being in England.

[An effusive reunion between two brothers] John Knightley made his appearance, and "How d'ye do, George?" and "John, how are you?" succeeded in the true English style, burying under a calmness that seemed all but indifference, the real attachment which would have led either of them, if requisite, to do every thing for the good of the other.—*Emma*

But Shakespeare one gets acquainted with without knowing how. It is a part of an Englishman's constitution. His thoughts and beauties are so spread abroad that one touches them everywhere; one is intimate with him by instinct.—Henry Crawford, in *Mansfield Park*

Beware of the insipid vanities and idle dissipations of the metropolis of England; Beware of the unmeaning luxuries of Bath and of the stinking fish of Southampton.—*Love and Friendship*

The truth is, that in London it is always a sickly season. Nobody is healthy in London, nobody can be. —Mr. Woodhouse, in *Emma*

One has no great hopes for Birmingham. I always say there is something dreadful in the sound.—*Emma*

Oh! Who can ever be tired of Bath!—*Northanger Abbey*

Kent is the only place for happiness, everybody is rich there.

Here's what may leave all painting and all music behind, and what poetry only can attempt to describe!—*Mansfield Park*

Admiration of landscape scenery has become a mere jargon.—Marianne Dashwood, in *Sense and Sensibility*

Over the mantel piece still hung a landscape in coloured silks of her performance, in proof of her having spent seven years at a great school in town to some effect.—*Sense and Sensibility*

She declared that she would give anything in the world to be able to draw; and a lecture on the picturesque immediately followed, in which his instructions were so clear that she soon began to see beauty in everything admired by him, and her attention was so earnest that he became perfectly satisfied of her having a great deal of natural taste. But now she should not know what was picturesque when she saw it.—*Northanger Abbey*

He talked of foregrounds, distances, and second distances—side-screens and perspectives—lights and shades; and Catherine was so hopeful a scholar that when they gained the top of Beechen Cliff, she voluntarily rejected the whole city of Bath as unworthy to make part of a landscape.—*Northanger Abbey*

"The walk is not good enough for our party. We had better take the avenue."

"No, no stay where you are, charmingly group'd. The picturesque would be spoilt by admitting a fourth. Goodby."—Elizabeth Bennett quips to Mr. Darcy, *Pride and Prejudice*

Everybody pretends to feel and tries to describe with the taste and elegance of him who first defined what picturesque beauty was.—*Sense and Sensibility*

I like a fine prospect, but not on picturesque principles.—*Sense and Sensibility*

It exactly answers my idea of a fine country, because it unites beauty with utility—and I dare—say it is a picturesque one too, because you admire it; I can easily believe it to be full of rocks and promontories, grey moss and brushwood, but these are all lost on me. —Edward Ferrars to Marianne Dashwood, in *Sense and Sensibility*

I have no knowledge in the picturesque, and I shall offend you by my ignorance and want of taste, if we come to particulars. I shall call hills steep, which ought to be bold! surfaces strange and uncouth, which ought to be irregular and rugged; and distant objects out of sight, which ought only to be indistinct through the soft medium of a hazy atmosphere. —Edward Ferrars, in *Sense and Sensibility*

ON NATURE & GREENERY

They are much to be pitied who have not been . . . given a taste for nature in early life.—*Mansfield Park*

To sit in the shade on a fine day, and look upon ver-
dure is the most perfect refreshment.—Fanny Price,
in *Mansfield Park*

In observing the appearance of the country, the
bearings of the roads, the difference of soil, the state
of the harvest, the cottages, the cattle, the children,
she found entertainment that could only have been
heightened by having Edmund to speak to of what
she felt.—*Mansfield Park*

ON THE WEATHER IN ENGLAND

I am sorry my mother has been suffering, and am
afraid this exquisite weather is too good to agree with
her. I enjoy it all over me, from top to toe, from right
to left, longitudinally, perpendicularly, diagonally;
nice, unwholesome, unseasonable, relaxing, close,
muggy weather.

ON FAMILY MATTERS

ON CHILDREN & MOTHERHOOD

Children

One does not care for girls till they are grown up.

The dear creature is just turned of two years old; as handsome as tho' 2 & 20, as sensible as tho' 2 & 30, and as prudent as tho' 2 & 40.

A family of ten children will be always called a fine family, where there are heads and arms and legs enough for the number.—*Northanger Abbey*

[On a nephew, then about three years old] I shall think with tenderness and delight on his beautiful and smiling countenance and interesting manner, until a few years have turned him into an ungovernable, ungracious fellow.

[To her sister, Cassandra, on the birth of another nephew] I give you joy of our new nephew, and hope if he ever comes to be hanged it will not be till we are too old to care about it.

If other children are at all like what I remember to have been myself, I should think five times the amount of what I have ever yet heard named as a salary [for a governess], dearly earned.—Emma, in *Emma*

Concession must be out of the question; but it was time to appear to forget that they had ever quarreled; and she hoped it might rather assist the restoration of friendship, that when he came into the room she had one of the children with her—the youngest.—*Emma*

I am losing all my bitterness against spoilt children, my dearest Emma.—*Emma*

One's heart aches for a dejected mind of eight years old.

Motherhood

A fond mother, in pursuit of praise for her children, the most rapacious of human beings, is likewise the most credulous; her demands are exorbitant; but she will swallow anything.—*Sense and Sensibility*

Poor woman! How can she honestly be breeding again? . . . I would recommend to her and Mr. D. the simple regimen of separate rooms.

Poor Isabella, passing her life with those [children] she doted on, full of their merits, blind to their faults, and always innocently busy, might have been a model of right feminine happiness.—*Emma*

And as for objects of interest, objects for the affections . . . the want of which is really the great evil to be avoided in not marrying, I shall be very well off, with all the children of a sister I love so much, to care about.—*Emma*

That I should be cautious and quick-sighted, and feel many scruples which my children do not feel, is perfectly natural; and equally so that my value for domestic tranquillity, for a home which shuts out noisy pleasures, should much exceed theirs.—*Mansfield Park*

Isabella always thinks as he [her husband] does; except when he is not quite frightened enough about the children.—*Emma*

She was a woman who spent her days in sitting, nicely dressed, on a sofa, doing some long piece of needlework, of little use and no beauty, thinking more of her pug than her children, but very indulgent to the latter when it did not put herself to inconvenience.
—*Mansfield Park*

She never knew how to be pleasant to children.
—*Mansfield Park*

Then, here come all my attempts at three of those four children; there they are, Henry and John and Bella, from one end of the sheet to the other, and any one of them might do for any one of the rest.—
Emma

Residing in the country without a family of children—having more than filled her favourite sitting-room with pretty furniture, and made a choice collection of plants and poultry—was very much in want of some variety at home.—*Mansfield Park*

In spite of maternal solicitude for the immediate enjoyment of her little ones, and for their having instantly all the liberty and attendance, all the eating and drinking, and sleeping and playing, which they could possibly wish for, without the smallest delay, the children were never allowed to be long a disturbance to him, either in themselves or in any restless attendance on them.—*Emma*

ON CHURCH, THE FAMILY & SOCIETY

It will, I believe, be everywhere found, that as the clergy are, or are not what they ought to be, so are the rest of the nation.—Edmund Bertram, in *Mansfield Park*

A sermon, well delivered, is more uncommon even than prayers well read.—*Mansfield Park*

A sermon, good in itself, is no rare thing.

A thoroughly good sermon, thoroughly well delivered, is a capital gratification.—*Mansfield Park*

I must confess being not always so attentive as I ought to be . . . nineteen times out of twenty I am thinking how such a prayer ought to be read, and longing to have it to read myself.—*Mansfield Park*

I wish you a better fate, Miss Price, than to be the wife of a man whose amiableness depends upon his own sermons.—*Mansfield Park*

I could not preach, but to the educated.—Edmund Bertram, in *Mansfield Park*

A man—a sensible man . . . cannot be in the habit of teaching others their duty every week, cannot go to church twice every Sunday, and preach such very good sermons in so good a manner as he does, without being the better for it himself.—*Mansfield Park*

Human nature needs more lessons than a weekly sermon can convey; and that if he [the preacher] does not live among his parishioners, and prove himself, by constant attention, their well-wisher and friend, he does very little either for their good or his own.

Mrs. Elton was first seen at church: but though devotion might be interrupted, curiosity could not be satisfied by a bride in a pew ... to settle whether she were very pretty indeed, or only rather pretty, or not pretty at all.

The obligation of attendance, the formality, the restraint, the length of time—altogether it is a formidable thing, and what nobody likes; and if the good people who used to kneel and gape in that gallery could have foreseen that the time would ever come when men and women might lie another ten minutes in bed, when they woke with a headache, without danger of reprobation, because chapel was missed, they would have jumped with joy and envy.—*Mansfield Park*

It is indolence ... Indolence and love of ease; a want of all laudable ambition, of taste for good company, or of inclination to take the trouble of being agreeable, which make men clergymen. A clergyman has nothing to do but be slovenly and selfish; read the newspaper, watch the weather and quarrel with his wife. His curate does all the work and the business of his own life is to dine.—Mary Crawford, in *Mansfield Park*

There is something in a chapel and chaplain so much in character with a great house, with one's ideas of what such a household should be! A whole family assembling regularly for the purpose of prayer is fine!—Fanny Price, in *Mansfield Park*

ON EDUCATION

A real, honest, old-fashioned boarding-school, where a reasonable quantity of accomplishments were sold at a reasonable price, and where girls might be sent to be out of the way, and scramble themselves into a little education, without any danger of coming back prodigies.—*Emma*

You might not give Emma such a complete education as your powers would seem to promise; but you were receiving a very good education from her, on the very material matrimonial point of submitting your own will, and doing as you were bid.—*Emma*

She . . . had no romantic expectations of extraordinary virtue from those for whom education had done so little.—*Emma*

His fortune was moderate and must be all his daughter's; but, by giving her an education, he hoped to be supplying the means of respectable subsistence hereafter.—*Emma*

Referring the education to her seemed to imply it. —*Emma*

Give a girl an education, and introduce her properly into the world, and ten to one but she has the means of settling well, without farther expense to anybody.—*Mansfield Park*

He knew her to be clever, to have a quick apprehension as well as good sense, and a fondness for reading, which, properly directed, must be an education in itself.—*Mansfield Park*

The politeness which she had been brought up to practise as a duty made it impossible for her to escape; while the want of that higher species of self-command, that just consideration of others, that knowledge of her own heart, that principle of right, which had not formed any essential part of her education, made her miserable under it.—*Mansfield Park*

Does our education prepare us for such atrocities? —*Northanger Abbey*

Hers is a line for seeing human nature; and she has a fund of good sense and observation, which, as a companion, make her infinitely superior to thousands of those who having only received "the best education in the world," know nothing worth attending to. —*Persuasion*

[On men] Education has been theirs in so much higher a degree; the pen has been in their hands. —*Persuasion*

There is, I believe, in every disposition a tendency to some particular evil, a natural defect, which not even the best education can overcome—*Pride and Prejudice*

Your mother must have been quite a slave to your education.—*Pride and Prejudice*

Why they were different, Robert explained to her himself. . . . he candidly and generously attributed it much less to any natural deficiency, than to the misfortune of a private education; while he himself, though probably without any particular, any material superiority by nature, merely from the advantage of a public school, was as well fitted to mix in the world as any other man.—*Sense and Sensibility*

Poverty is a great evil; but to a woman of education and feeling it ought not, it cannot be the greatest. —*The Watsons*

Fraternal love, sometimes almost every thing, is at others worse than nothing.—*Mansfield Park*

Children of the same family, the same blood, with the same first associations and habits, have some means of enjoyment in their power, which no subsequent connexions can supply; and it must be by a long and unnatural estrangement, by a divorce which no subsequent connexion can justify, if such precious remains of the earliest attachments are ever entirely outlived.—*Mansfield Park*

When her mother could be no longer occupied by the incessant demands of a house full of little children, there would be leisure and inclination for every comfort, and they should soon be what mother and daughter ought to be to each other.—*Mansfield Park*

Never could I expect to be so truly beloved and important; so always first and always right in any man's eyes as I am in my father's—*Emma*

What strange creatures brothers are! You would not write to each other but upon the most urgent necessity in the world; and when obliged to take up the pen to say that such a horse is ill, or such a relation is dead, it is done in the fewest possible words. You have but one style among you . . . "Dear Mary, I am just arrived. Bath seems full, and every thing as usual. Yours sincerely." That is the true manly style; that is a complete brother's letter.—*Mansfield Park*

Nobody, who has not been in the interior of a family, can say what the difficulties of any individual of that family may be.—*Emma*

On the Human Condition
on aging

If I live to be an old woman I must expect to wish I had died now, blessed in the tenderness of such a family, and before I had survived either them or their affection.

Anne hoped she had outlived the age of blushing; but the age of emotion she certainly had not.—*Persuasion*

It sometimes happens that a woman is handsomer at twenty-nine than she was ten years before; and generally speaking, if there has been neither ill health nor anxiety, it is a time of life at which scarcely a charm is lost.—*Persuasion*

His notice of me—"a pleasing-looking young woman"—that must do; one cannot pretend to anything better now; thankful to have it continued a few years longer!

By the bye, as I must leave off being young, I find many douceurs in being a sort of chaperone for I am put on the sofa near the fire and can drink as much wine as I like.

Sickness is a dangerous indulgence at my time of life.

Mr. Lyford says he will cure me, and if he fails I shall draw up a Memorial and lay it before the Dean and

Chapter, and have no doubt of redress from that pious, learned and disinterested body.

ON ENVY

You will not ask me what is the point of envy.
—*Emma*

Be honest and poor, by all means—but I shall not envy you; I do not much think I shall even respect you.—*Mansfield Park*

I never listened to a distinguished preacher in my life without a sort of envy.—*Mansfield Park*

Lucy, who, though really uncomfortable herself, hoped at least to be an object of irrepressible envy to Elinor.—*Sense and Sensibility*

ON NEUROSIS

Nobody is on my side, nobody takes part with me, I am cruelly used, nobody feels for my poor nerves.
—Mrs. Bennet, in *Pride and Prejudice*

You mistake me, my dear. I have a high respect for your nerves. They are my old friends. I have heard you mention them with consideration these twenty years at least.—Mr. Bennet to Mrs. Bennet, in *Pride and Prejudice*

Always some little objection, some little doubt, some little anxiety to be got over.—*Mansfield Park*

She is a poor honey—the sort of woman who gives me the idea of being determined never to be well and who likes her spasms and nervousness and the consequence they give her, better than anything else.

Troubles and ill-health having, of course, the same origin . . . —*Emma*

She would not be so weak as to throw away the comfort of a child, and yet retain the anxiety of a parent!—*Sense and Sensibility*

[In 1817, asked if there was anything she wanted]
Nothing but death.

One does not love a place the less for having suffered
in it, unless it has been all suffering, nothing but suffering.—*Persuasion*

We met. . . . Dr. Hall in such very deep mourning
that either his mother, his wife, or himself must be
dead.

ON PITY

My sore throats are always worse than anyone's.
—*Persuasion*

Those who do not complain are never pitied.—Mrs.
Bennet, in *Pride and Prejudice*

Perhaps, sir, I thought it was a pity you did not always
know yourself as well as you seemed to do at that moment.—Fanny Price, in *Mansfield Park*

The indignities of stupidity, and the disappointments of selfish passion, can excite little pity.—*Mansfield Park*

She had received ideas which disposed her to be courteous and kind to all, and to pity every one, as being less happy than herself.—*Persuasion*

He is such a charming man, that it is quite a pity he should be so grave and so dull.—*Sense and Sensibility*

ON VANITY

Vanity working on a weak head produces every sort of mischief.

To come with a well-informed mind is to come with an inability of administering to the vanity of others, which a sensible person would always wish to avoid.

Vanity and pride are different things, though the words are often used synonymously. Pride relates more to our opinion of ourselves, vanity to what we would have others think of us.

To be the favourite and intimate of a man who had so many intimates and confidantes, was not the very first distinction in the scale of vanity.

Vanity was the beginning and the end of Sir Walter Elliot's character; vanity of person and of situation.
—*Persuasion*

It is very often nothing but our own vanity that deceives us.

Their vanity was in such good order that they seemed to be quite free from it, and gave themselves no airs; while the praises attending such behaviour, secured and brought round by their aunt, served to strengthen them in believing they had no faults.
—*Mansfield Park*

He had vanity, which strongly inclined him in the first place to think she did love him, though she might not know it herself; and which, secondly, when constrained at last to admit that she did know her own present feelings, convinced him that he should be able in time to make those feelings what he wished.—*Mansfield Park*

Had I really loved, could I have sacrificed my feelings to vanity, to avarice?—*Pride and Prejudice*

The world had made him extravagant and vain— extravagance and vanity had made him cold-hearted and selfish.—*Pride and Prejudice*

Vanity while seeking its own guilty triumph at the expense of another, had involved him in a real attachment, which extravagance, or at least its offspring, necessity, had required to be sacrificed.—*Pride and Prejudice*

JANE AUSTEN
(1775–1817)

Jane Austen was raised in two very different worlds: the quiet country life of her native Hampshire village and the stormy narrative world of the eighteenth-century novel. In Steventon, England, she was the daughter of the rector, a gentile scholar who urged learning in each of his eight children. Her mother was a writer—within the family at least—applying her ready wit to impromptu verses, and stories. Acting and novel reading were great family amusements.

And what fun the Austen children must have had reenacting those contemporary dramas, in which women were victim to fainting spells and men to the mystique of a pretty girl or a picturesque landscape. Jane Austen mocked the sentimental fiction of her day as a precocious teenager; in her journal she sketched scenes wavering between burlesque humor and brutal commentary. As a mature writer, Austen substituted irony for mockery, and morality and common sense for the violent and overt emotion of her early parodies.

In Austen's published novels, it is noticeably the heroine who must save herself. Not unlike the young Jane's struggle to break free from a spell cast by silly novels, the title character of *Emma,* Marianne Dashwood in *Sense and Sensibility,* Catherine Morland in *Northanger Abbey,* and Elizabeth Bennet in *Pride and Prejudice* must realize the deceit in their own girlish dreams to find love and happiness in the course of the novel.

And real, practicable love was always the point of the novel. While it's true that all Austen books climax in marriage, their plots are more tangled around women attaining maturity than husbands. And as Austen heroines struggle with their growing emotions, they must do so against the demands of family and society. Husbands abound as just reward for striking a balance between good sense and romantic sensibilities. Husbands with whom they can share love, but also who can support them in a world in which they could not support themselves.

This truth about money and marriage Jane Austen knew only too well. To her unmarried sister

Cassandra she quipped, "Single women have a dreadful propensity for being poor." Likewise poor women had a propensity for remaining single. Austen's own "portionless" circumstance may have put an abrupt end to an early romance with a Steventon neighbor. She was eventually proposed to at age twenty-nine, but would not accept for fear of a marriage without love. By her early thirties Jane had seen enough of babies and birthing to appreciate her lack of them (the wives of two brothers each died while giving birth to their eleventh child). By refusing conjugal ties, she had in effect chosen to live out her life as the dependent of her brothers.

Success as a novelist could never change her dependency on the Austen men. The most successful runs of her novels netted her little more than one hundred pounds per year, covering only one-fourth of her expenses. Perhaps more important, for Austen, her ability to write depended upon a settled home that only men could provide. Under her father's eye at Steventon Jane was a prolific writer. She arrived at her twenty-fifth birthday with three novels written: "Elinor and Marianne" (which became *Sense and Sensibility*), "First Impressions" (later *Pride and Prejudice*), and "Susan" (published posthumously as *Northanger Abbey*). Her novel writing came to a halt when her father the Reverend George Austen retired from his curacy and relocated his family to Bath. Distanced from the gentry and clergy of rural England in urban Bath, she lost contact with those she wrote almost exclusively about. The change from a house to a family apartment no doubt would have robbed the aspiring writer of her cherished privacy. Or maybe it was Bath itself that disheartened her enough to surrender her aspirations. Whatever the cause, she wrote little.

Within five years of leaving Steventon, her father died leaving Jane alone in Bath and obliged to accept whatever living arrangements the Austen men chose for her. For ten years she lived in the homes of her brothers and other family members and produced almost nothing new.

She eventually resumed her rhythm of work after her brother Henry settled her and her mother into a cottage in Chawton, a sleepy village of sixty families much more like the settings of her youth and earlier novels. Their red-bricked home sat at a fork in the road. Built probably as a posting inn, passers-by could see into the rooms of Chawton Cottage. Likewise, Jane Austen could see out.

She dug up the manuscript of "Elinor and Marianne," then a novel in letters, and began revisions. Initial attempts to interest publishers in her work failed, but her brother Henry came through for her using his wife's money and his old army connections. In 1810 Thomas Egerton of the Military Library agreed to publish *Sense and Sensibility* on commission; Henry paid for the printing, advertising, and distribution of the book in an agreement that allowed for Jane to keep the copyright.

Sense and Sensibility was an instant success. Published in late 1811, it was sold out by the summer of 1813. For her next novel, *Pride and Prejudice* (1813), Egerton was ready to pay. While not widely known or acclaimed, Austen was read in fashionable circles. The Prince Regent himself enjoyed her books so much that his librarian asked Austen to dedicate a later novel to him. Sir Walter Scott also gave her favorable reviews.

Public interest in her novels might well have been raised by a curiosity to know their author. Austen published her first two books anonymously, since literary airs were not something a lady wished to be accused of. But in time the rumors of her authorship spread too far to discount.

Mansfield Park appeared on the book market in May 1815. Published without much fanfare, it included Jane's name on the title page. Author status, however unladylike, in this case gained her a reputation for morality. Public praise for the character of Fanny Price was so strong it somewhat reduced the reception of her novel from entertainment to edification.

Austen's publisher, Egerton, did not think *Mansfield Park* as good as her previous novels and although it did sell out, he made no plans for a second printing. The Austen family's reaction to her new book was also less enthusiastic. One family member described Fanny as "insipid," and all generally agreed that she was not so engaging as Elizabeth Bennet in *Pride and Prejudice.*

Within a year, Jane broke ties with Thomas Egerton and the Military Library. A new publisher accepted *Emma* for publication (1816), and agreed to produce a new revised edition of *Mansfield Park.* The revised book was a failure in terms of sales, but the new *Emma* proved her most successful work to date. A far cry from the morally perfect Fanny Price, the title character of Emma was selfish and calculating, yet likable. Unlike Fanny who waits for her moral strength to be discovered, Emma asserts her own will. The greater depth of characterization in *Emma,* and the use of dialogue to develop those characters, is especially evocative of Austen's growth as a novelist.

Jane's very productive years at Chawton were not without personal setbacks. Her sister-in-law and early patron, Eliza, died of breast cancer. Eliza's husband Henry became entangled in a legal suit in 1814 that threatened to halve his fortune and force his sisters and mother out from Chawton Cottage. By the time Jane stopped working on her next novel, *Persuasion,* she had succumbed to an unknown illness that eventually proved fatal.

Written in the last few years of her life, *Persuasion* is a novel about aging. It is a romance for women, like the author, who could not help but fantasize about a second chance for happiness in love and life. Of all her novels, it is her most clear evocation of how merit can rise to dissuade any perceptions of diminishing beauty in the heroine. *Persuasion* offers up Austen's usual irony and witty epigrams, but its overall mood is more serious, more reflective.

Persuasion remained unpublished during Austen's lifetime, but we can gather from the author's letters that she regarded it as "ready for publication." The same cannot be said for *Sandition,* an unfinished novel for which she wrote twelve chapters between January and March 1817.

Jane Austen died on 17 July 1817, leaving her sister and lifelong confidante Cassandra as executrix of her estate and copyright holder of her novels. Five months after her death, Cassandra published both *Persuasion* and one of Jane's earliest novels, the gothic satire *Northanger Abbey.*

Jane left no diaries. While some of her letters were preserved, Cassandra destroyed the bulk of those. A niece did the same with letters kept by one of Jane's brothers. The author's legacy and, in a sense, the many sides of her character draw from her famous creations. She is survived by Elizabeth, Elinor and Marianne, Fanny, Emma, Catherine and Anne. As the imaginative offspring of their author, these voices offer subtle yet stunning glimpses into the mind and spirit of a truly great English writer.